Old MID & EAST CALDER

Including KIRKNEWTON and OAKBANK

by

William F. Hendrie

Calder Hall was situated between Mid Calder and East Calder. It belonged to the Hare family, whose graves lie in the burial ground beside the ruins of St Cuthbert's Church in East Calder. The fine two-storey Georgian-style mansion was demolished in the late 1970s. All that now remains is the tree-lined drive, which is located to the south-west of the village.

ACKNOWLEDGEMENTS

My thanks to Kirknewton local historian Thomas Hardie; Revd John Povey; headmaster of St Paul's Primary School, Gerry O'Brien; former headmaster of Kirknewton Primary School, Gilbert Donaldson; West Lothian Countryside Ranger, Mary Konik; West Lothian Local History Librarian, Sybil Cavanagh; and the many other people of the Calders area who patiently answered my various questions.

The publishers would like to thank Ian Hossack for providing the pictures on pages 7, 9, 10, 11, 15, 17, 28, 32, 36 and 37.

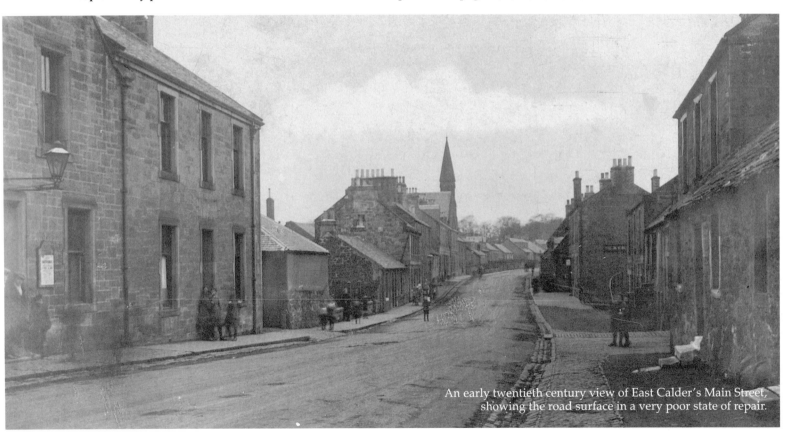

An early twentieth century view of East Calder's Main Street, showing the road surface in a very poor state of repair.

INTRODUCTION

East, Mid and West Calder are situated to the west of Edinburgh and south of the new town of Livingston, within view of the Pentland Hills. Originally within the county of Edinburghshire, as it was once known, all three of the Calders became part of West Lothian under Scottish local government reorganisation implemented in 1975 following recommendations made by Lord Wheatley. The Calders remained in West Lothian following further reorganisation of local administration on 1 April 1995. This book focuses on East and Mid Calder and the nearby villages of Kirknewton and Oakbank; a companion volume deals in detail with West Calder.

The Calders are attractive small towns which share a name derived from two Celtic words – *coil* and *dour* – meaning 'the well watered woods'. The watery aspect of the definition is appropriate as three rivers merge near Mid Calder, with the Linhouse and Murieston Waters flowing into the more major River Almond. The latter meanders north, forming the eastern boundary of West Lothian before finally joining the River Forth at Cramond.

The area occupied by the Calders was originally divided between two estates: Calder Clere, where East Calder is now situated, and Calder Comitis (meaning the Earl's Calder) where Mid Calder and West Calder are sited. King Malcolm IV granted the former estate to Randulph de Clere in 1160 and the latter belonged to the Earl or Thane of Fife, who features in Shakespeare's 'Scottish play', *Macbeth*.

As early as the twelfth century a church at the west end of East Calder was dedicated to St Cuthbert, a saint associated with the east coast who had connections with both Lindisfarne and Durham. Annual tithes from St Cuthbert's were paid to the monks of Kelso Abbey. In 1215 Duncan, Thane of Fife, gave money to build a church on his estate at Mid Calder. This was enlarged in 1542 as a result of a gift of £3,000 from its then rector, Peter Sandilands, whose descendants still own Calder House. There is a long-standing connection between the Sandilands and Mid Calder dating back over seven centuries and originating when the Barony of Calder Clere was forfeited during the Scottish Wars of Independence. King Robert the Bruce subsequently bestowed it upon James, 1st Earl of Douglas, from whom the Earls of Morton are descended and who take their title from Mortoune, a place-name found in the Calders area. James in turn gave the Barony of Calder to his sister Eleanor, Countess of Carrick, upon her marriage to James de Sandilands in 1349 and this gift was subsequently given the royal seal of approval by King David II.

Further royal recognition of Mid Calder followed when James, son of James de Sandilands, married the daughter of King Robert II in 1384 and the monarch paid a royal visit to Calder House. The Sandilands were also prominent in the affairs of the Knights of the Order of St John of Jerusalem, and in 1539 Sir James Sandilands succeeded Sir Walter Lindsay as head of the Knights Hospitallers in Scotland and preceptor of Torphichen Preceptory. Sandilands' period of office coincided with the Reformation (1560), and as the demise of Roman Catholicism posed a threat to the Knights' estates, he astutely avoided their seizure by surrendering them voluntarily to Mary, Queen of Scots. The grateful monarch later returned the lands around Torphichen to Sandilands as a secular grant, and to celebrate this he took the title of Lord Torphichen.

During the turbulent years of the Reformation, Calder House played an important role in Scottish religious affairs as it was while the key Protestant figure John Knox was a guest there in 1556 that he conducted what was possibly the first Holy Communion according to the reformed rite. The dynamic Knox also took the opportunity to preach to the people of Mid Calder on several occasions, addressing the crowds which thronged Market Street. So many people wished to hear him that instead of preaching in the church alone he also delivered sermons in the open air, shielded from the elements by a large tree behind the kirk.

The best-known of Mid Calder's ministers were the two John Spottiswoods. John Spottiswood Snr. was appointed rector of Mid Calder around 1548 by Sir James Sandilands. Educated at Glasgow University, Spottiswood travelled to London following his graduation where he studied the reformed doctrines of Archbishop Cranmer – thus when the Reformation came to Scotland he supported the Protestant cause. As a result he was made Superintendent of the Lothians, Merse and Teviotdale.

His son John was born at Greenbank, Mid Calder in 1565 and became even more famous. John Jnr. also attended Glasgow University and when he graduated, aged only eighteen, was appointed assistant to his father at Mid Calder, later succeeding him. His eloquence in the pulpit and knowledge of Protestant doctrine brought him to the attention of King James VI, and at the Union of the Crowns in 1603 he became one of the 'Hungry Scots' – so-called because they were said to be eager for office – who accompanied the monarch to London. At the royal court Spottiswood was indeed rewarded when James VI of Scotland and I of England created him Archbishop of Glasgow. With the introduction of episcopacy in 1610, Spottiswood was promoted again, becoming Scotland's senior churchman, Archbishop of St Andrews. His patron, King James, died in 1625 and it was eight years before Charles I travelled north for his Scottish coronation. The ceremony took place at Holyrood Palace in 1633, where the crowning was performed by Spottiswood. Despite this, John Spottiswood subsequently fell out of favour and because of his views was excommunicated by the Church in 1638. He returned to England where he died in 1639 and was buried in Westminster Abbey.

Six years later, during the summer of 1645, the inhabitants of Mid Calder were forbidden by the Kirk Session to go to Edinburgh because plague had broken out in the city. Two local men, James Gairdner and Alan Shaw, defied the ban and were sentenced to imprisonment in the stocks in Market Street. In autumn farm workers were banned from changing jobs at Martinmas (11 November) – as they did by custom at that time – in order to reduce the risk of plague spreading throughout the area. Instead labourers were ordered to continue working for their masters at their existing wages until the frosts of winter eventually brought the outbreak to an end.

Around the same time the Calders district was affected by an entirely different kind of fever in the form of fear of witches. Allegations were made about some (mainly elderly) women of the Calders being in league with the Devil and practising witchcraft. The minister of Mid Calder Parish Church in 1644, the Revd Hew Kennedie, took the role of witch-finder upon himself, leading an investigation which resulted in several Mid Calder women being arrested. The accused were tried and found guilty, and at least one of them, Agnes Bishop, was strangled to death at the stake by the executioner. Her body was then carried to the top of Cunnigar Hill where it was burned on a huge bonfire. Strangely-shaped Cunnigar is believed to be topped by a Bronze Age tumulus or burial barrow and derived its unusual name at a later date as a result of the rabbit warrens which honeycombed its steep sides (*cuniculus* is Latin for rabbit, and cunnigar is a Scots word meaning rabbit warren). The hill has never been the subject of a full archaeological excavation, but Stone Age coffins have been unearthed nearby.

Following the execution of King Charles I in 1649, Oliver Cromwell's Republican army marched through the Calders in 1650 and his soldiers camped overnight at West Calder. After the restoration of the monarchy with the accession to the throne of King Charles II in 1660, the Calders were the scene of much support for the Covenanters. As a result government dragoons under the command of General Tam Dalyell of the Binns came to the area in November 1666 to suppress these religious rebels. The troops established a camp, but despite the general's efforts – which earned him the nickname of 'Bluidy Tam' – the Covenanters continued to hold their secret conventicles, worshipping in the open air on the slopes of the Pentland Hills rather than submitting to the Episcopalian worship imposed by King Charles II. Tam Dalyell, Member of Parliament for Linlithgow and currently Father of the House of Commons (being its longest-serving member, but due to stand down in 2004), is descended from General Tam Dalyell.

Government forces remained unpopular and in 1684 two soldiers, Life Guards Thomas Kennoway and Duncan Stewart, were found murdered at nearby Swine Abbey. Both men had been notorious for their severity towards those who wished to pursue their own style of worship, and they were believed to have beaten an elderly man in Mid Calder suspected of attending a service in the hills. A court of inquiry was convened at Mid Calder Parish Kirk, but despite the interrogation of the local population those who had murdered the soldiers were never apprehended.

More positively, the reign of Charles II also saw the passing of an Act of Parliament authorising two fairs to be held annually in Mid Calder. These were important events, because as well as facilitating the sale of animals and produce they were also occasions at which farm labourers could offer themselves for hire, and many potential employees from the surrounding area flocked to Mid Calder seeking work. As a result the Calder fairs also attracted travelling folk from across Scotland, who set up stalls to entertain the crowds and encourage them to part with their money.

The Calders remained rural communities throughout the eighteenth and the first half of the nineteenth centuries. Significant developments in agriculture took place during the mid-eighteenth century, bringing changes to the appearance of the fields and farms in the district. These changes are described in the first *Statistical Account*, for which West Calder's entry was written in 1796 by the Revd John Muckersy, known locally as 'yon clever wee body'. To clear the moss from the land, the improvers required large quantities of lime (whose alkaline properties acted as a fertiliser), and this led to the opening of limekilns at East Calder.

Apart from these kilns, the only other industrial activity in the Calders took the form of a few small coal pits and stone quarries, plus several mills powered by the waters of the River Almond. The East and West grain mills in Mid Calder Parish were amongst the more important of the mills. East Mill provided flour for sale locally, while the West Mill, later known as Wallace Mill, had a wider market selling flour and oatmeal as far afield as Glasgow. At first its products were transported to the city by horse-drawn cart, but following the opening of the Union Canal in 1822 some cargoes were delivered by barges (again horse-drawn) and later by the new railways which came to the area in the 1840s. Other mills in Mid Calder included the waulk mill, where cloth was fulled (cleansed and thickened), and New Calder Mill. The latter manufactured paper and still operates, although nowadays produces cardboard tubes.

It was, however, the Scottish shale oil industry which completely changed the Calders district in the second half of the nineteenth century.

James 'Paraffin' Young patented the production of oil from the mineral torbanite (defined as 'a variety of algal or boghead coal from Torbane Hill, Scotland, which on distillation gives a high yield of oil'), and later from reserves of shale which were available in abundant supply below the ground around the Calders. Young brought his wife and family to live at Limefield House, near Polbeth, between Mid and West Calder while he supervised the building of the world's first oil refineries, shortly before the oil boom in America. The profits of their products – one of which was paraffin, which provided a safe fuel for household lamps and earned Young his nickname – helped finance the expeditions to Africa of his former classmate at Glasgow's Andersonian Institute, Dr David Livingstone. While spending time in Scotland between his missionary endeavours, Livingstone had a holiday with Young and his family at Limefield and entertained the children by building an imitation African kraal in the grounds. In honour of his distinguished guest, Young had his labourers dam the stream which flowed through the garden at Limefield to form a miniature Victoria Falls. Livingstone had been the first white man to observe the real falls, which he named after Queen Victoria.

Mid Calder was only modestly affected by the booming oil industry, with a few managers' homes being built there (these now form part of the town's conservation area). Industrialisation approached the town in the shape of Oakbank village, which was built on the estate of Calder Hall specifically to house the influx of shale miners and their families. These families occupied the long, low, crowded lines of cheaply-constructed homes known as miners' rows.

Looming over the rows were the ever-growing vast pink plateaux of spent shale, the only by-product of the Scottish oil industry for which Young could not find a constructive use. These giant bings dramatically changed the appearance of the countryside around the Calders, and now the most famous group of these man-made mountains, the Five Sisters, has been officially listed as a monument to the Scottish oil industry and is depicted on the coat of arms granted by the Lord Lyon, King of Arms, to West Lothian Council. The latter was established in 1975 as a district council, and following the abolition of regional councils in 1996 has been responsible for all local government services for the Calders area.

Following the cessation of the shale oil industry in 1962 the Calders suffered a period of decline, but are now prospering again. East, Mid and West Calder are all proving popular with newcomers who find the small towns attractive places in which to make their homes while travelling daily to work in Edinburgh and Glasgow. Oakbank has essentially been erased from the map following the demolition of its rows in 1984, but like the Calders, Kirknewton is now a popular and attractive dormitory settlement. It is hoped that this book will be of as much interest to incomers to these districts in finding out more about where they have chosen to live and raise their families as it will be to residents who have dwelt there for the whole of their lives.

East Calder's Main Street was devoid of traffic when this postcard view looking east was produced in the early 1900s. Then as now the scene is dominated by the lofty spire of the parish church, which was erected in 1886 at a time when the local economy was booming as a result of the development of the shale oil industry. Most of the buildings in the picture still stand, including Springfield Cottage, situated adjacent to the church and bearing a date-stone indicating it was built in 1889. The houses directly opposite the church have been demolished and their site is now occupied by East Calder's library, although the two-storey stone villa to the west of the library (out of sight in this view) remains in place and is now the showroom for Hann Furnishing.

Langton Road

Copyright

Arched Gateway

Lilywhite Ltd.

Post Office Corner.

Main Street.

EAST CALDER
E.C.8.

Bridge & River.

East Calder is the closest to Edinburgh of the three Calders, and its broad Main Street is glimpsed twice in this multiview postcard. The central picture shows what is known as Post Office Corner, while the lower left view looks east past the parish church towards the city. The houses in the picture at the top left stand in Langton Road which leads from East Calder to Kirknewton. They were built following the First World War by Mid Lothian County Council as part of central government plans to improve housing standards and were made available for rent at economic rates. During the Second World War prefabs were also built in East Calder and in the post-war years the Scottish Special Housing Association added to the number of new homes in the town. Despite these building projects, East Calder retains a comparatively rural aspect and this is reflected in the other two pictures, both showing well-known local landmarks. One is the impressive gateway at the entrance to what was originally the private estate belonging to Almondell House, now open to all as Almondell and Calderwood Country Park. The other shows the graceful Nasmyth Bridge, which spans the River Almond and has been restored as another of the park's many attractive features.

THE CHURCH YARD, EAST CALDER.

St Cuthbert's Parish Church is first mentioned in records dating from the twelfth century and was dedicated in the early 1240s by David de Bernham, Bishop of St Andrews, in whose diocese it lay. The roofless, ivy-covered ruin shown in this picture probably dates from the sixteenth century. When Kirknewton and East Calder parishes united in 1750, a new church was built in the former village, but in 1776 a group of seceders constructed a United Presbyterian Church in East Calder – today this building serves as the church hall. A more modern United Presbyterian Church was built in East Calder in 1886, becoming a United Free Church in 1901. In 1929 its congregation, along with many others across Scotland, decided to reunite with the Church of Scotland from which it had separated following the Disruption of 1843. A union was forged with Kirknewton Parish Church in 1943, thus appropriately reuniting the territory covered by the original Kirknewton and East Calder parishes. This union continues to the present day, with one minister serving both villages from the manse in Manse Place, East Calder.

A group of workers and the company horse (a vital member of any business that involved transporting goods or people in the early years of the twentieth century) gather on East Calder's Main Street outside the premises of Martins Hygenic Bakery adjacent to the forestair seen in the lower picture. The premises on the corner were occupied by Andrew Millar, butcher.

Looking west along Main Street in the years before the First World War when the only traffic in evidence was a lone horse-drawn cart. The photograph appears to have been taken from where the car park of The Grapes is now situated. A well-known local hostelry, The Grapes opened its doors in 1895 and has been a popular focal point in East Calder ever since. The curved forestair in front of the house on the right is an attractive feature of this early view.

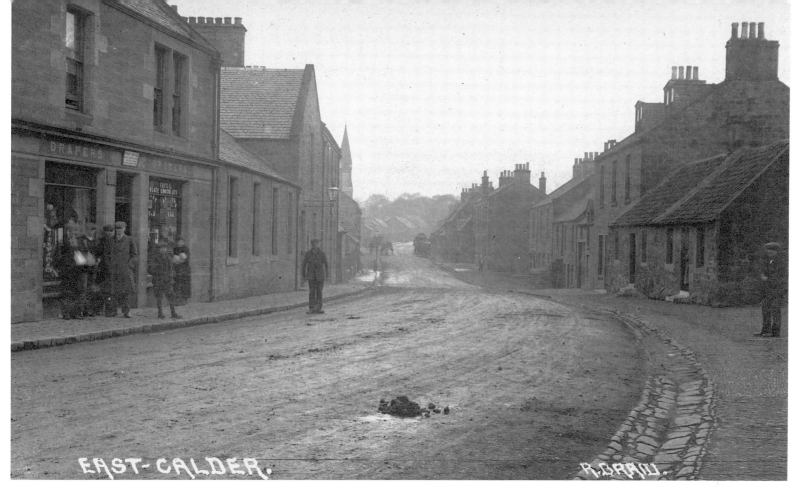

EAST-CALDER.

R.BRAW.

Stark's drapers was one of the busiest shops in East Calder, and its enterprising owners later opened a grocery department too, as seen here. This vied for custom with the grocers operated by West Calder Co-operative Society. The society was founded in 1875 with capital of £4,588, all in £1 shares owned by local members. Beyond Stark's is the pointed gable of the building used as an early village school, and whose premises are now occupied by the Community Education Department. East Calder's first school was also located in Main Street and incorporated the headmaster's house on the first floor. The building which replaced it still stands on the south side of the street and is now used as a community hall, while the neighbouring School House serves as a play school for the village's youngest children. The present East Calder Primary School was originally opened in 1936 as a joint primary and junior secondary. The secondary department was closed in 1965 with the introduction of the comprehensive education system, and its pupils were transferred to the larger and more modern premises of West Calder High, to which older pupils from East Calder still travel by bus each day.

East Calder's other school is St Paul's Roman Catholic Primary, whose original premises are illustrated here. These were situated in Kilronan Park at the east end of the village behind St Theresa's Church, in what is now its car park. The old St Paul's was demolished in 1964 following the opening of a new school. This was built by Mid Lothian Education Authority and based on what was known as the Lothian Model, a modular design which in its day was considered a highly successful blueprint for primary school buildings. With an assembly hall, stage and kitchen at its core, it was designed so that wings of classrooms could be added from any side, and the steady increase in the number of pupils attending St Paul's has necessitated the construction of two such extensions. At the time of writing it has a roll of 145 pupils aged from four to twelve, with 26 younger children in its nursery class. As has been the case throughout its history, St Paul's caters for pupils from a wide catchment area with five minibuses bringing children in each day from places including Currie, the southern edge of Livingston and Mid Calder. It is because the boys and girls attending it have traditionally come from so many different parishes that the school bears a different name from St Theresa's Church, with which it nevertheless maintains a close pastoral relationship. The present St Theresa's was erected in 1935.

Traditionally pupils from St Paul's Primary School participated in an annual fête day, similar to those held by churches in France. Wearing white communion dresses, the girls held banners depicting the saints while the boys, dressed in scarlet and white surplices, headed the procession with the priest as it proceeded around Kilronan Park. In this picture the children are passing the Presbytery, the priest's residence in the village.

Situated in spacious grounds in Kilronan Park at the east end of East Calder, the Presbytery was – and still is – a very visible symbol of how prominent a position the Roman Catholic community occupied in the town's life. Its numbers were greatly strengthened by the arrival of many Irish immigrants attracted to the area by the jobs available in the local shale mines and oil industry during the nineteenth century. The Presbytery is still home to the priests who serve the surrounding Roman Catholic parish.

POST OFFICE CORNER, EAST CALDER. E.C. 3.

Main Street at Post Office Corner. The batteries of chimney pots are a reminder that practically all of East Calder's homes were once heated by coal fires, for which fuel was delivered in hundredweight sacks carried on horse-drawn carts. While horse-drawn vehicles remained a common sight until after the Second World War, at least one motor lorry had already appeared on the scene by the time this postcard was produced, probably in the 1930s.

West End, East Calder.

A canopy of trees overarches Main Street in this photograph taken at the west end of East Calder looking east towards the spire of the Parish Church. The road through the village was formerly part of an important route between Edinburgh and Glasgow.

The two-storey building on the right of this picture of Main Street formerly housed a Masonic Hall, and the pediments of its three windows bear carvings representing the thistle, rose and clover. The former hall has now been converted into houses.

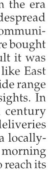

A group of girls pose for a photograph on Main Street while other children and some adults look on. Most of the illustrations in this book are reproduced from Edwardian postcards, which in the era before telephones became widespread were an important means of communication. Millions of postcards were bought and posted daily, and as a result it was quite normal for a small town like East Calder to be represented on a wide range of cards featuring most of its sights. In the first half of the twentieth century there were numerous postal deliveries every day except Sunday, and a locally-addressed postcard sent in the morning could confidently be expected to reach its destination by teatime at the latest.

ALMONDELL VIADUCT. EAST-CALDER.

The massive nine-arch Camps Viaduct (wrongly referred to as Almondell Viaduct on this postcard) was constructed in 1885 to carry a branch line to Pumpherston Oil Works from the North British Railway's main line. This branch also served a quarry, brickworks and one of East Calder's limekilns at the hamlet of Camps. The viaduct has been preserved and now forms part of a popular high-level walk in Almondell and Calderwood Country Park.

Almondell and Calderwood Country Park has a linear layout which follows the course of the River Almond from Mid Calder to Lin's Mill and the Almond Aqueduct on the Union Canal. Along its route the park features several bridges of interest, one of which is a smaller aqueduct which was constructed between 1818 and 1822 to supply water to the Union Canal. The bridge illustrated here was designed by artist and architect Alexander Nasmyth and built c.1800 to carry one of the main drives to Almondell House. Nasmyth (1757–1840) was well-known as a painter of both landscapes and portraits, with one of his most famous subjects being Robert Burns. Among the other bridges nearby is an ultra-modern A-frame suspension bridge which was built shortly after the opening of the park in 1970 to provide access to the east bank of the Almond. The A-frame was flown in by helicopter in two sections. These were then welded together on site before being hoisted into position, while the deck was carefully inched out on rollers until in position over the river. The result is one of the most unusual suspension bridges in Scotland, similar in appearance to the Erskine Bridge over the Clyde, although on a smaller scale.

Almondell and Calderwood Country Park's headquarters and visitor information centre is housed in the former stables of Almondell House. However, whilst the stables' classical facade has been preserved, the beautiful country mansion seen in this photograph was demolished in 1969. It had been built in 1789 for the Hon. Henry Erskine, whose distinguished legal career included twice becoming Scotland's Lord Advocate: first in 1782 and again in 1806. Born in 1746, the year of the Battle of Culloden, Erskine was the second son of the 10th Earl of Buchan and brother of Lord Chancellor Thomas Erskine, who became the first Baron Erskine of Restormel. Henry was known as the 'poor man's friend' because it was said that as a young lawyer he never turned down a case, even when he knew that the client was too poor to pay his fees. During his lifetime Almondell House was the setting for many of Scotland's most colourful social events. Henry Erskine was reckoned to be the outstanding wit and orator of his age, and his good humour often carried over into his work in court. A famous contemporary, Lord Jeffrey, noted that Erskine's illustrations were always a delightful feature of his cases, but were also always a material step in the reasoning of the matters before the court. Erskine retired in 1811 to enjoy the pleasures of his East Calder estate, including fishing the waters of the Almond and its tributaries the Murieston and Linhouse Waters. After his death in 1817 he was succeeded by his son, who became Lord Cardross and 12th Earl of Buchan. Almondell remained the family seat for well over a century, the last member of the family to occupy it being the dowager Countess of Buchan who lived there until her death in 1943. The house stood a short distance south-west of the visitor centre and its foundations now lie below one of the car parks. The stone pillar in front of the visitor centre was originally erected around 1700 in the grounds of another of the Erskine family's properties, Kirkhill, which still stands near Broxburn. The inscriptions on it were part of a miniature scale model of the solar system, which Henry Erskine's elder brother, David, 11th Earl of Buchan, designed.

This garage was situated at Raw Camp on the outskirts of East Calder and sold several brands of petrol including Pratts, BP and Shell, as was typical in the days before most petrol stations became tied to a particular supplier. It's not known who this well turned-out group are, but the smart motor vehicle, with AA badge on its radiator grille, may have been chauffeur-driven by the uniformed man on the left. Safety regulations on garage forecourts were once much more relaxed than they are today, as evidenced by the chauffeur's cigarette. East Calder's lime industry was formerly based near where the garage stood at Raw Camp. The limekilns stood on part of the Earl of Morton's estate and were established following the agrarian revolution in Scotland in the middle of the eighteenth century to provide supplies of lime for use as a fertiliser. There was originally a windmill adjacent to the kilns, and the Morton estate records show that around the year 1814 a steam engine was installed. Both these sources of power were used to pump water (probably from the quarries from which the limestone was extracted), and the steam engine was also harnessed to feed lime into the tops of the ever-hungry kilns. The lime produced was shovelled on to waiting horse-drawn carts to be delivered to local farmers.

Some of the petrol produced by the Scottish shale oil industry (located at Philpstoun) was sold under the brand 'Scotch' and dispensed from distinctive thistle-topped pumps such as this one.

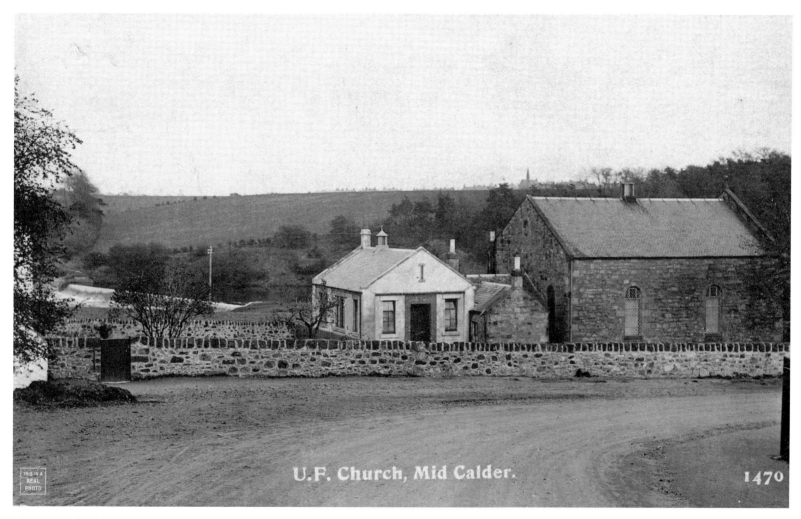

U.F. Church, Mid Calder.

1470

THIS IS A REAL PHOTO

The austere building that became Mid Calder United Free Church traced its history to 1761 when a Presbyterian denomination called the Associate Presbytery seceded from the Church of Scotland. The church – described as a 'meeting house' – was built in 1765 at Bridgend. In 1847 a number of secession churches came together to form the United Presbyterian Church, and it was at that point that the church illustrated here became Mid Calder UP Church. In 1901 it became a United Free Church when the UP and Free Churches united.

New Bridge and Glen Almond, Mid Caulder.

The 'New Bridge' was built to carry the main road from Pumpherston to Mid Calder over the River Almond.

In this picture the tall chimney of the West or Wallace Mill is seen emerging from the wooded depths of Glen Almond. This mill produced meal and its output latterly consisted of feed for farm animals. At one time there were four mills in Mid Calder, all powered by the water of its rushing streams. Now only New Calder Mill is in production, and today this is powered by electricity. Owned by the Wyllie family from 1763 (when it opened) for over 200 years, it produced various kinds of paper, latterly using waste newsprint as its raw material. Having been acquired by Adam Robertson & Co., the mill was sold to Limehouse Boards in 2003, and although still trading under the name of Robertson, production has been switched to making cardboard tubes for various industrial uses.

PARISH CHURCH, MID CALDER. R.BRAID. Photo.

Like the church in East Calder, Mid Calder's kirk was dedicated by Bishop David de Bernham who performed the ceremony on 14 March 1241. The church was extended in 1863 and the organ installed in 1888. An interesting feature is that the building has two entrances, the second of which was used by Lord Torphichen and his family to gain access to the prominently-raised pew which was the town's equivalent of a lairds' loft. Despite its modernisation in 1863, the church retains many earlier features including the spiral turnpike or newel stair which leads to the belfry. The alterations of the 1860s included the removal of a wall which had been built across the chancel arch and the addition of a transeptal extension designed by Maitland Wardrop, of well-known Edinburgh architects Brown & Wardrop. Several masons' marks are to be found in the church, devices that were originally carved by workmen to ensure that they were paid for the work which they had done, and which are said to give rise to the expression 'piece work'.

Built in the nineteenth century, the manse illustrated here was home to successive ministers of Mid Calder Parish Kirk until its replacement by a new house in the 1920s. Like its predecessor, this has since been superseded by the present manse in Maryfield Park, which was acquired by the congregation in 1983. On several occasions in the parish's past, Mid Calder's minister adopted the role of witchfinder-general when cases of local women reputedly trafficking with the Devil were reported to the Kirk Session. These cases arose between the end of the sixteenth century and the early eighteenth century. Having been found guilty in February 1644, at least one local woman, Agnes Bishop, was publicly executed by being strangled at the stake before her body was burnt. Two other alleged witches were Jean Anderson, who was sentenced to be imprisoned in sackcloth, and Margaret Thomson, who was also imprisoned but subsequently released having complained that the then minister, Revd Hew Kennedie, had deprived her of sleep for twenty days. The last recorded case of witchcraft occurred in 1720 when twelve year-old Patrick Sandilands, the third son of Lord Torphichen, appeared to suffer from hallucinations and went into trances. It was thought that he had been bewitched by several local women, who were arrested but subsequently released after young Master Sandilands recovered. The 40 acre glebe that surrounded the manse was of ample size to be used for grazing, and the revenue generated thereby formed part of the minister's income. Generally speaking clergy leased their glebes rather than undertaking the farming of them themselves.

MID-CALDER, FROM THE WEST. FB.

Mid Calder's handsome Parish Kirk, featured in *Churches to Visit in Scotland* (the book published as part of the Scotland's Churches Scheme), is on the left of this view showing the approach to the town from the west. There is known to have been a place of worship in Mid Calder since the reign of King David I in the first half of the twelfth century, when a church was established by local landowner the Earl of Fife. Whilst those accused of witchcraft merited particular – and often extreme – punishment, lesser miscreants, such as those who missed church on several Sundays or committed fornication out of wedlock, might be sentenced by the elders of the Kirk Session to sit on the tall wooden Seat of Repentance. This was set in front of the pulpit of Mid Calder Parish Kirk in view of the whole congregation. Also known as the 'Cutty Stool', it is now in safe keeping at Calder House.

Quite appropriately, Mid Calder's Bank Street is dominated by the imposing Victorian bank building seen in the centre of this picture on the left. Bank Street was also the location of the town's post office and co-operative store, the latter being operated by West Calder Co-operative Society. Outside the store, on the edge of the pavement, stood a gas lamp, a reminder that Mid Calder had its own gasworks of which the name Gasworks Brae is a lasting reminder. In the background the curved facade of Main Point can be glimpsed.

CHURCH STREET, MID CALDER, FROM THE WEST

Over the years Mid Calder's Main Street has been known variously as Street of Calder, High Street and Church Street, and it is the latter name that appears on this postcard. Most of the buildings seen here date from the mid to late nineteenth century, although the small whitewashed cottage on the right was older. The street narrowed towards its far end, and this stretch was known quaintly amongst locals as 'the techt (tight) bit'. The premises of the Black Bull Inn, established in 1749, can be seen in the distance facing the camera.

The two-storey terrace on the right-hand side of Church Street (Main Street) in this view was built by local artist William Penny, and was always known as Penny's Buildings. It was demolished in the 1960s and replaced shortly afterwards by local authority housing. Mid Calder's two most historic houses are the eighteenth century Brewery House, which takes its name from the brewery on the site of which it stands, and Calder Bank, which was built *c*.1775.

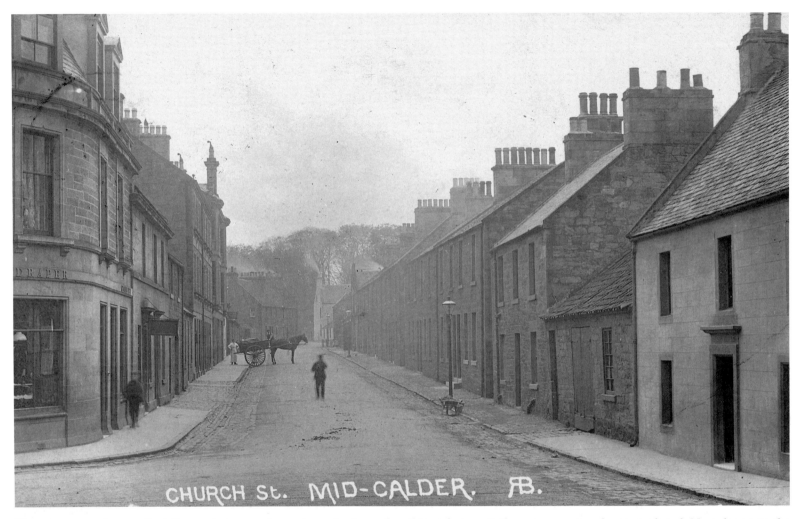

CHURCH St. MID-CALDER. AB.

The corner premises on the left were being used as a draper's shop when this early twentieth century postcard was produced. Next door was the stationer's belonging to Mr Gilchrist, which sold a series of postcards depicting views of the town and surrounding district. Today these premises are occupied by the lawyers and estate agents, Peterkin & Kidd. All of the buildings on the right-hand side of Mid Calder's Main Street, as seen in this picture, have been demolished, apart from the house in the distance with white harled walls.

Picturesque Combfoot (often known as Camfoot) was in Mid Calder and stood on the road to Pumpherston. The attractive collection of buildings was demolished many years ago.

THE DRY-BRIDGE. MID-CALDER. R. BRAID

The 'Dry Bridge' – so-named because it crossed a road rather than a watercourse – carried the private driveway to Lord Torphichen's Calder House over the public road and enabled his guests to reach the house without using the main street through Mid Calder. Once a well-known local landmark, it was demolished in 1949 because it was proving a hazard to the increased volumes of traffic using the road, particularly SMT buses on local services which were forced into the centre of the carriageway to pass under it.

The property of Lord Torphichen, Calder House is first mentioned in 1335 and has belonged to the Sandilands family (of which he is a member) since the Middle Ages. The family derive their name from the lands which they originally owned in Clydesdale. Calder House, which was extended in 1700 and again in 1780, is situated about 100 metres south of Mid Calder Parish Kirk. Until the end of the eighteenth century the houses of the original village stood near it, but at that point Lord Torphichen decided to improve his estate by demolishing the cottages and rebuilding them where Mid Calder is now situated. He takes his title from the village of Torphichen fifteen miles to the north in the Bathgate Hills, where the Knights of the Order of St John of Jerusalem had their Scottish headquarters until the Reformation. At that time one of his ancestors, James Sandilands, was the preceptor of the order. The Torphichen family burial vault lies below Mid Calder Kirk.

"CATHER FAIR"   BANK ST. MID-CALDER.

The width of Mid Calder's Bank Street made it ideal for both regular markets, and – more importantly – the twice-yearly Calders or Cauther Fair. This dated from the reign of Charles II and attracted crowds of labourers and servants who came to offer their services to the area's farmers. These local holidays were known as feeing fairs, and when a deal was struck it would be sealed with a handshake and the handing over of a silver coin by the farmer.

The largest building in Market Street is the former Working Men's Institute, seen on the left in this picture. Containing a reading room and various recreational facilities, the hall was an important gathering place in Mid Calder during Victorian times. After being closed for several years, it was reopened in June 1994 and a plaque on the exterior of the building indicates that funds were provided by Mid Calder Inter Pub and Club Talent Contest Fund. Perhaps less beneficial to the moral fibre of the town than the institute were the nine inns and pubs for which Market Street was renowned, and which were particularly crowded with drinkers on the two annual fair days. The Black Bull Inn is visible on the right of this picture.

As well as being a place of revelry on market days and at Cauther Fairs, Market Street was where wrongdoers were publicly punished. Some were flogged – receiving a prescribed number of strokes inflicted by a leather lash – whilst others were locked in the wooden stocks. A third and distinctly Scottish mode of public penance were the jougs. A joug was an iron collar (attached by a chain to an immovable object) which would be locked around the neck of an offender and which the Kirk Session had the power to sentence minor miscreants to wear for a set number of hours. Mid Calder's jougs were attached to the huge plane tree which was a feature of Market Street for several centuries. In 1793 local minister Revd Dr Wilson estimated the girth of its trunk to be eighteen feet and reckoned that its branches stretched out over twenty feet. The tree was damaged by a storm in 1829 and its stump and the iron jougs which were attached to it were removed in 1860.

Main Point has been a prominent landmark in Mid Calder since the middle of the eighteenth century. It first appears on a map of 1763, although the curved gable was added at a later date. Initially the main road between Edinburgh and Lanark ran to the north of the building, but when a new bridge over the River Almond was built in 1794 to avoid steep hills and make access easier for stagecoaches, the new road passed Main Point to the south, as it still does today. Traffic for Pumpherston, Uphall and other destinations to the north continued to use the old road (seen on the left in this picture) into the nineteenth century. Main Point has housed many businesses over the years and was home to Swan's sweetie shop when this photograph was taken. The sign of the Torphichen Arms juts into the top right-hand corner of this picture of Main Point.

The Torphichen Arms is labelled the Lemon Tree Inn on the map of 1763. This was a busy coaching inn which formed the first stopping point on journeys between Edinburgh and Glasgow and Edinburgh and Ayr. In 1838 Mid Calder's minister, the Revd John Sommers, wrote that 'Besides the mail there is a daily coach between Edinburgh and Glasgow, another between Edinburgh and Ayr and on every alternate day there is one between Edinburgh and Hamilton, all of which pass through Mid Calder. On the south or Carnwath Road is a daily coach from Edinburgh to Lanark during the summer months and every alternate day in winter . . . ' While passengers enjoyed a refreshment at the inn, the horses which pulled the stagecoaches were either watered or changed for a fresh team at the stables opposite, reached through the pend whose arched entrance can still be seen on the north side of the street.

HUNT MEETING • MID CALDER. AB.

Horses were very much in evidence when the hunt met in Mid Calder prior to the chase. This picture shows members of the Linlithgow and Stirlingshire Hunt enjoying a stirrup cup outside the Torphichen Arms, with the hounds waiting for the horn to herald the beginning of the day's work. The hunt dated back to 1763 and was disbanded in 1991 when it was banned from operating over local authority owned land. The increasing volume of traffic on even minor roads was another contributory factor in its demise.

MID-CALDER FROM THE BRIDGE. ÆB.

The approach to Mid Calder via the bridge from the east. All the buildings in this picture still stand, including the Masonic Hall in Hall Street, which belongs to the members of Lodge St John No. 272.

Members of Mid Calder Athletic Football Team, which won the McCulloch Cup in the 1922/23 season. The names of the players have been pencilled faintly on the reverse of the photograph:

Back row: Samson, Hands, White, Maywood, Turnbull
Third row: McLaughlan, Cairns, Preston, Peden, Wallace, Stark, Clarkson, Wynne
Second row: McCriner, Clarkson, Nelson, McLeann, McGinty, McBurnie, Russell
Front row: Armstrong, Watson

Kirknewton's current church opened for worship in 1750, replacing an earlier building situated in the middle of the village. The original long, low primary school building (in use until 1924) is also seen in this picture. Until the end of the eighteenth century the minister also filled the role of dominie, teaching the bairns their lessons on weekdays in addition to preaching to his congregation on Sundays. The old school had no indoor plumbing and even on the coldest of winter days the boys and girls had to run across the playground to use outside toilets. Children from many surrounding hamlets – and farms as far afield as the foothills of the Pentlands – walked every morning to attend school in Kirknewton, and former pupils still recall how these country bairns often arrived clutching hard-boiled eggs which they used as hand-warmers on the long hike to their classes. At lunchtime these formed part of their packed lunches! The old school still rings with the sound of children's voices as it now houses the local pre-school play group.

Kirknewton's substantial manse provided a home for the minister, his wife and their family. This attractive villa still stands in the village.

Kirknewton's Smithy Brae was alive with children when Robert Braid took this photograph in the early years of the last century. Smoke wafted from the chimneys of the houses, and the forge at the smithy would have added to the smoky atmosphere. The blacksmith's shop was located on the left-hand side of the short, steep street and gave it its name. As well working as a farrier, the smith also made iron implements for local farmers and often repaired the metal rims of their cartwheels. There are still metal rings in the walls of several local buildings where horses were formerly tethered. Kirknewton Inn, in the middle of the village, was a regular stopping place for the drovers who herded cattle south from the Highlands via the trysts at Falkirk and Larbert. They paused at the inn before continuing their slow journey through the Cauldstane Slap in the Pentland Hills and on over the border to English markets where the cattle were eventually sold. Stagecoach passengers also patronised the inn on their journeys to and from Edinburgh and Lanark. Transport in the area was, however, revolutionised in 1847 by the opening of Kirknewton railway station. This is still the busiest place in the village on weekday mornings and evenings, as local commuters use the railway to travel to work in both Edinburgh and Glasgow as well as Livingston, one of whose stations, Livingston South, is served from Kirknewton. Many villagers live in houses which were built in the 1950s to accommodate service families based at the nearby army and air force bases, whose influx doubled the population of Kirknewton at the time.

LINBURN, WILKIESTON

Linburn Estate, located at Wilkieston near East Calder, was purchased to provide sheltered accommodation for blind and partially-sighted servicemen in July 1944 by the Scottish National Institution for the War Blinded, a charity which was established in 1915 by the directors of the Royal Blind Asylum in Edinburgh. The mansion as seen in these pictures was demolished c.1954 following the completion of new purpose-built premises within the grounds of the 100 acre estate. In addition to sheltered housing, these originally included a hostel, but this closed in 2001 as support at home for residents became more viable and popular. Workshops continue to be run at Linburn for the manufacture of teak summer seats, whilst other garden furniture is also made in materials including wrought iron.

Linburn is named after a nearby small stream, but it is in fact the Gogar Burn which flows through the grounds, part of which have now been sold to provide a public park for Wilkieston. Linburn's superintendent, Leslie Meikle, has worked here for the Scottish National Institution for the War Blinded in various roles since 1966, and the estate's head gardener, George Nicol, also joined the staff in the same year and has served for three months longer.

These miners' rows once lined both sides of Main Street in Oakbank. The village was built in 1864 on the estate of Calder Hall, midway between Mid and East Calder, to house workers at the newly-opened Oakbank Oil Co.'s works. A total of 165 houses were initially erected and the cost of renting them was deducted weekly from the miners' and other workers' wages. The census of 1871 recorded that the population of Oakbank totalled 355, but during the next two decades the number of miners and their families staying in the village increased rapidly, and by the time of the census of 1891 had almost tripled to reach 979 people. The recession of the 1920s had a major effect on Oakbank, and its oil works were closed down in 1932. From then on the number of families living in the village dwindled until it became virtually deserted. All of the remaining rows were demolished in 1984.

Quilting was a popular winter activity amongst the members of Oakbank Women's Rural Institute who are proudly displaying some finished examples of their work in this photograph. The village also had a Burns Club, as well as bowling, football, golf and rifle-shooting clubs. The village institute, bowling club and a loft for racing pigeons are all that now survives of this once flourishing mining community.

Kirknewton House, originally called Meadowbank, was the home of well-known Edinburgh legal figure Lord Maconochie, who tried notorious murderer William Burke of Burke and Hare fame, sentencing the accused to be hanged in the Grassmarket. William Hare escaped a similar fate by turning king's evidence (giving evidence for the prosecution). Having been reduced in size by the demolition of one of its wings, Kirknewton is now the attractive home of the Welwood family, whilst its stable block and part of the spacious grounds are used by Maximillion, a corporate events company, for outdoor adventure activities which are offered as part of its popular management training courses. Maximillion has its headquarters at nearby Overton Cottage.

THE SWANS
KIRKNEWTON HOUSE

These swans were a popular feature in the grounds of Kirknewton House, although the poorer members of the village community seldom got the opportunity to see them as the mansion and its grounds were generally only accessible on the annual open day, which was usually held on a summer Saturday. In winter this pool – which was linked to a second pond by a short stretch of water known as the canal – served another useful purpose, with slabs of ice being cut from its frozen surface and stored in the mansion's ice house. Ice houses were insulated underground chambers which were filled with ice in winter. If managed carefully, the supply could be made to last all year round and ice would then be available for cooling purposes in the kitchen even in the height of summer.

This ornate statue and the pond it overlooks are still attractive features in the grounds of Kirknewton House. The estate also includes a walled garden.